The Ghost of Genny Castle

JOHN ESCOTT

Level 2

Series Editors: Andy Hopkins and Jocelyn Potter

Pearson Education Limited
Edinburgh Gate, Harlow,
Essex CM20 2JE, England
and Associated Companies throughout the world.

ISBN 0 582 41800 3

First published by Penguin Books 1995
Published by Addison Wesley Longman Limited and Penguin Books Ltd. 1998
New edition first published 1999

5 7 9 10 8 6 4

Typeset by RefineCatch Limited, Bungay, Suffolk
Set in 11/14pt Monotype Bembo
Printed in Spain by Mateu Cromo, S.A. Pinto (Madrid)

Published by Pearson Education Limited in association with
Penguin Books Ltd., both companies being subsidiaries of Pearson Plc

For a complete list of the titles available in the Penguin Readers series please write to your local
Pearson Education office or to: Marketing Department, Penguin Longman Publishing,
80 Strand, London WC2R 0RL

Contents

Introduction

Claire looked across the fields and saw a tall stone building. 'An old castle!' she said. 'I must go and see that before I go home again.'

Aunt Min didn't look at the castle. 'It – it's not a nice place to visit,' she said. 'Genny Castle is dangerous.'

'Dangerous?' said Claire. 'Why?'

When Claire's mother and father go away for Christmas, Claire goes to stay with her Aunt Min. Aunt Min lives in the village of Little Genny and near it is an old castle. Claire is very interested in the castle and she wants to know more about it. But the people in the village are afraid of Genny Castle and they won't talk to her about it. Accidents happen there. People die . . .

Aunt Min says she must stay away, but Claire knows she can't. She must find answers. And soon, she will. Because in the castle something is waiting. And it *knows* her.

John Escott writes books for students and young people. He was born in a small country town in Somerset, in the south-west of England. Now he lives in Bournemouth, by the sea. He is married and has two children. When he is not writing, he likes walking and he plays music.

He wrote *The Ghost of Genny Castle* after he saw a *real* old dark castle: Corfe Castle in Dorset, England. This is near his home town. Corfe Castle is nearly one thousand years old and people there tell a lot of stories about it.

You can also read *Detective Work* and *Money to Burn* by John Escott in Penguin Readers.

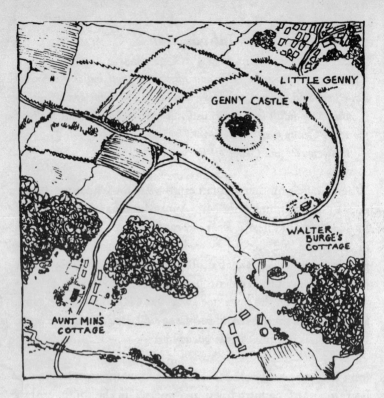

Aunt Min's Cottage, Walter Burge's Cottage,
Genny Castle and Little Genny.

Chapter 1   The Castle

It was a cold December afternoon. Walter Burge was outside his cottage when he saw the car in the road, across the fields. It was Minnie Dawe's car.

'Who's *she* taking home?' thought Walter. 'A visitor?'

Walter didn't like visitors. 'Stay away from the castle,' he told them when they came in the summer. Sometimes they didn't listen to him. But this was winter, when not many people came.

He watched the car for a minute or two, then he went back to his work.

◆

An orange cat was outside the cottage. It was the colour of fire. It too watched the car. Then it walked slowly across the field at the back of the cottage and up to Genny Castle.

◆

Claire looked out of the window of the little car.

'Is it far to your cottage, Aunt Min?' she asked.

'About six miles,' said her aunt.

The village of Little Genny was behind them now, and snow began to fall from the grey December sky. Claire thought about Christmas. 'It's going to be nice here with Aunt Min,' she thought.

'The last time I saw you was ten years ago,' said Aunt Min.

'I was only five years old then,' said Claire with a laugh.

'And now you're as tall as me,' said Aunt Min. She was tall and thin with grey hair. 'Where did your mother and father go? I can't remember.'

'New Zealand,' said Claire. 'They went because of Dad's job, and they're coming back in January.'

Aunt Min smiled. 'And you're going to be with me in my little cottage for Christmas,' she said.

Claire smiled back, then she looked across the fields and saw a tall stone building.

'An old castle!' she said. 'I must go and see that before I go home again.'

Aunt Min didn't look at the castle. 'It – it's not a nice place to visit,' she said. 'Genny Castle is dangerous.'

'Dangerous?' said Claire. 'Why?'

Aunt Min didn't answer. She looked across the field at the old building and said, 'Stones are always falling from the walls and towers.'

Claire looked at her aunt. 'There's something Aunt Min isn't telling me,' she thought. 'What is it? Does the castle have a secret?'

◆

When Claire got up the next morning the sun was in the sky.

'Did you sleep well?' asked Aunt Min.

'Yes, very well,' said Claire.

After breakfast Aunt Min said, 'I must go to the church in Little Genny this morning. Do you want to come with me? You can look round the village.'

'OK,' said Claire.

An hour later they drove to Little Genny. There was some snow on the fields and the castle was beautiful. '*Is* it dangerous?' thought Claire.

Her aunt stopped the car in the village.

'I can walk up to the church and meet you later,' said Claire.

She wanted to get her aunt something for Christmas, and after Aunt Min drove away she went into a small shop. It sold

'An old castle!' Claire said. 'I must go and see that before I
go home again.'

books, pictures, writing-paper and envelopes, and a lot of other things.

'Aunt Min likes writing long letters to her friends,' thought Claire. 'I can get her some writing-paper and envelopes.'

She looked at the books. 'Do you have a book about the castle?' she asked the woman in the shop.

'No,' said the woman, 'we don't.'

'Is there a picture of it that –?' Claire began.

'No,' the woman said quickly.

Claire bought a book about old churches, then paid for the writing-paper and envelopes before she went outside.

'What's wrong with Genny Castle?' she thought. 'Nobody likes to talk about it. Why?'

◆

It was good to be out in the sun again, and Claire went for a walk round the village. It was a very pretty place, with a lot of small cottages and a little school. The church was at the top of one of the roads.

Claire was near the church when a big old car stopped in front of her. A man got out. He wore a long, heavy coat and his hair was thick and grey. He carried a shopping-bag in one hand. Some women were outside the shop, but they moved away quickly when they saw the man. He went into the shop.

'Nobody likes Walter Burge,' somebody said.

Claire turned round and saw a boy behind her.

'Why?' she asked.

'I think they're afraid of him,' said the boy. He was about three years younger than Claire. He wore jeans and a warm coat.

'Why?' Claire asked again.

The boy put a finger to his head. 'Crazy,' he said. 'They think old Walter is crazy. Perhaps he is. He lives in the cottage near the castle.'

4

'Do you have a book about the castle?' Claire asked the
woman in the shop.

Some women were outside the shop, but they moved away quickly when they saw Walter.

'What's wrong with the castle?' said Claire.

The boy looked round, but there was nobody listening. 'It's a bad place,' he said. 'Bad things happen there. My dad sometimes talks about it.'

'What *things* happen at the castle?' Claire asked. 'I really want to know.'

'Accidents,' said the boy. 'Some years ago a woman died there. Some of the tall tower – the Black Tower it's called – fell down. She was under it.'

Claire thought for a minute, then she said, 'Accidents can happen. A place isn't *bad* because accidents happen there.'

'*She* does it!' said the boy.

'"She"?' said Claire. 'Who's "she"?'

'The ghost,' the boy said quietly.

'Ghost?' said Claire. She laughed.

'Don't laugh!' said the boy. He was angry. 'People in the village don't talk about it.' And he walked away.

'Ghosts!' Claire thought. She smiled. 'That *boy* is crazy, not the old man. I'm going to see that castle before I go home. But perhaps it's better to say nothing to Aunt Min. I don't want to worry her.'

Claire opened the door of the church and went inside. She saw her aunt and some other women with flowers in their hands. She watched them put the flowers round the building.

Aunt Min saw her. 'We're getting it ready for Christmas Day,' she said.

'The flowers are beautiful,' said Claire.

'There's an evening of Christmas singing here tomorrow,' Aunt Min said, 'for the people in the village.'

'Can we come?' said Claire.

'Do you want to?' said her aunt.

'Yes,' said Claire.

Aunt Min smiled. 'Good, because I do too,' she said. 'Did you have an interesting morning?'

Claire remembered the old man – Walter Burge – and the boy.

'Yes,' she said. 'Very interesting.'

Chapter 2   The Witch Story

After lunch Claire said, 'I'm going for a walk.'

'Don't get lost,' Aunt Min told her.

There was a cold wind, and it got colder when she arrived at the castle field. But it was a nice, sunny afternoon – an afternoon to laugh at stories about ghosts, she thought.

Claire saw the cottage and she saw Walter Burge outside it again. His car was near the cottage. She did not want him to see her, so she moved across and up the field quickly. From time to time she looked back at the cottage. It got smaller and smaller as she got closer to the castle.

Soon she was near the dark towers. There was no sun here and it was very cold. Everything was quiet. There were no sounds of birds or animals.

The cottage was far below her. 'I'm OK now,' she thought. 'He can't see me.'

She went over to the tallest tower – the Black Tower, the boy called it. Did the woman die here? There was a door at the bottom. Inside, stone stairs went up to the top.

Suddenly Claire was afraid. 'Why am I afraid?' she thought. 'Ghosts?'

Then she heard a sound.

She thought it was a bird and looked up quickly . . .
. . . *and a big stone fell from the top of the tower.*

Something in her head said *MOVE!* Claire jumped away and

8

. . . and a big stone fell from the top of the tower.

threw herself down. The big stone hit the bottom stair and broke, and for a minute or two Claire could not move.

Another accident? said something in her head.

She looked up at the top of the tower. Somebody . . . some-*thing* was up there! What was it? It had a head the colour of fire. But was it a man or a woman? Or was it a bird? Claire waited for it to fly down.

And then it was not there.

♦

Walter Burge heard the stone fall and looked up at the castle. His face was white and he was afraid. He saw somebody running down the field.

'Stop!' Walter called. 'Stop!'

But the girl ran on, too fast for Walter's old legs to catch her.

♦

Claire ran back to Aunt Min's cottage.

'Is that you, Claire?' said Aunt Min.

'Yes,' Claire answered. She waited at the back door for a minute before she went into the room at the front of the cottage.

'Claire!' said Aunt Min, looking at her. 'What's wrong? Your shirt is all dirty.'

'I – I fell over,' said Claire. 'Don't worry, I'm OK.' She tried to smile.

'Come and sit down,' said her aunt. 'Let's have a cup of tea.'

Claire sat down in a chair. Then she saw something in the corner of the room. 'You've got a Christmas tree!'

Aunt Min smiled. 'The day after tomorrow is Christmas Day, remember,' she said. 'I brought it in from the garden and put it up when you went for your walk. Do you like it?'

'Yes!' said Claire, laughing now.

'There are some lights to go on it,' said Aunt Min. 'I think

Claire found a very old book. It was small and thin

they're in the little room at the top of the stairs. Perhaps you can look for them in the morning.'

'OK,' said Claire.

♦

Much later, when Claire went to bed, she thought about the castle again.

'I'm not going back,' she thought. 'Genny Castle can have its secrets. I don't want to know them.'

♦

The next morning Claire went up to the little room at the top of the stairs. There were a lot of boxes in the room, two old chairs, a desk with a broken leg and a big cupboard. The Christmas tree lights were in the cupboard. Claire found them easily.

She saw some books at the back of the cupboard. Most of them were stories, but then Claire found a very old book. It was small and thin, and she read the words on the front of it: *The Story of Genny Castle*.

'Did you find the lights, Claire?' Aunt Min called from the bottom of the stairs.

'Yes,' Claire said.

She put the book inside her shirt. 'I don't want Aunt Min to know that I have it,' she thought. 'Why?' But she did not have an answer to her question.

Later that morning she went to her bedroom and began to look at the book. There were pictures of the castle and stories about people. These people lived at the castle many years ago. Some were famous, some were good, and some were bad.

Suddenly Claire saw a word.

Witch.

She began to read.

♦

'She's going to die!' the man said.
'Who can help her?'

A woman came to the castle about two hundred years ago. She was a servant. Where did she come from? Nobody asked her, but soon after she came things began to go wrong. Servants were ill. Animals began to die. Everybody at the castle was afraid. 'What's happening?' they asked.

'It's the new servant!' somebody said. 'She's a witch!'

'A witch, yes!' said the others. 'She must die! Burn her!'

The man living at the castle had a daughter. She was fifteen years old. One day she too was ill.

'She's going to die!' the man said. 'Who can help her?'

'The witch can help her,' his servants told him. And they brought the woman to him.

'Please help my daughter!' the man said to the witch.

'No!' she said. 'It's right for your daughter to die. You burned my sister three years ago!'

'No!' said the man.

'You lived at a different castle then, and my sister and I were two of your servants,' said the woman. 'My sister, Alexa —'

'Alexa!' said the man. 'I remember! I remember her because she was a witch too! She was dangerous, so we burned her. And you are her sister?'

'Yes,' said the witch. 'I watched somebody I loved die. Now you are going to watch your daughter die.'

'No, please!' said the man. 'Help her!'

'Never!' said the witch.

And a week later the girl died.

After that, they took the witch to the top of the Black Tower and burned her.

Today, people say that they see and hear the ghost of the witch on the tower at midnight. They say that they see her fire-coloured hair and her green eyes.

◆

Claire stopped reading. She did not want to know any more.

. . . *they took the witch to the top of the Black Tower and
burned her.*

Chapter 3   An Accident in the Snow

Claire and her aunt drove to the church that evening. There was a strong wind and snow started to fall again. Claire watched it through the car window. But she did not think about the snow or about Christmas: she thought about the witch and about the fire-coloured *thing* that she saw on the top of the Black Tower after the stone fell. These thoughts stayed with her all evening and she only half-listened to the singing in the church. She could not get the story of the witch out of her head.

When the Christmas singing was finished, she and Aunt Min went back to the car through the snow. Now it came up over their shoes, and the night was very cold.

The car made lines in the snow when they drove away from the church, and everything was white – white houses, white trees, white cars, people's white coats. Soon they were in the little roads outside the village and there were no other cars, only Aunt Min's. Driving was difficult. The car could not stop easily in the snow. Aunt Min drove carefully, but with a worried face.

They were in the road near the castle. Aunt Min tried to drive slowly – but the car went faster and faster in the snow!

'I can't stop it!' she said.

And then the car went off the road and hit a tree!

Aunt Min put her hands to her face and shut her eyes.

'Are you OK?' Claire asked.

'Y-yes, I think so,' said her aunt.

They got out of the car and looked at it.

'I can't drive it now,' said Aunt Min. 'I must phone the garage in the village. Mr Perkins can drive out and see it tomorrow. But now we must get home, Claire.'

Claire looked across the fields. She could see Genny Castle. Aunt Min looked at the castle too and Claire could read her

And then the car went off the road and hit a tree!

aunt's thoughts: it was more than two miles round the road, but it was not a mile across the fields.

'Let's go across Walter Burge's field,' said Aunt Min. 'I can't walk all round the road.'

She got a light from inside the car, then they went into the field and began to walk through the snow.

Claire tried not to look at the castle.

◆

Walter Burge sat in a big chair in front of the fire in his cottage. There was a book about castles in his hands. There were other books in the little room and many of them were about castles too.

His cat, Alexa, sat by the fire.

Walter knew the stories that people in the village told about him. 'He's crazy,' they said, and he knew this. And he knew the stories about the castle. People said it was a bad, dangerous place. He didn't try to stop these stories, because people stayed away when they heard them, and Walter didn't want people to go near the castle. He knew that the castle had its secrets.

He stopped reading and closed his eyes.

Alexa, the cat, stood up. She walked into the kitchen without making a sound, and across to a window. The window was not quite shut and she pushed it with her foot. When it was open, Alexa jumped down into the snow.

She began to walk up to the castle.

◆

Walter opened his eyes. 'It's time I went to bed, Alexa,' he said.

Then he saw that the cat was not there, and he got up out of the chair and walked through to the kitchen.

'Alexa?' he said. He saw the open window. 'Again?' he said. 'Why did you go out on a night like this?'

When the window was open, Alexa jumped down into the snow.

Walter knew that the cat went up to the castle. He remembered other nights – nights when people in the village heard sounds and saw lights on the Black Tower. Nights when Walter shut his cottage doors and stayed inside.

Walter tried not to think about these things. He loved his castle, but he knew that the village people were worried about it. 'The castle is a bad place,' they said. 'Pull it down!' Walter did not want that to happen.

'I must stop you, Alexa,' he said.

And he took a light from a cupboard, pulled on his shoes and coat, and went out of the back door, into the snow and the wind.

◆

'I'm so cold,' Claire thought.

She and Aunt Min walked across the field. They could see Walter Burge's cottage, half a mile away. Claire was worried about her aunt. How far could she walk in the snow? The old woman's face was grey and she was very, very tired.

Claire took the light from Aunt Min, then put a hand under her aunt's arm. She helped her across the field to Walter Burge's cottage.

'We must stop here for you to sit down, Aunt Min,' Claire said above the sound of the wind.

Her aunt was too tired to say anything.

The front door of the cottage was shut, but Claire hit it with her hand. 'Mr Burge!' she called. There was no answer. She tried to open the door, but it stayed shut. 'Let's go round to the back,' she told her aunt.

They went round to the back door of the cottage. Claire looked at the snow by the door. 'He's gone out,' she thought. 'I can see his footprints in the snow; they're going up to the castle. But what is he doing up there?'

Claire took the light from Aunt Min, then put a hand under her aunt's arm.

There was no time to think about this – her aunt was cold and tired. Claire pushed open the back door of the cottage and they went inside.

They found the room with the fire and Aunt Min sat on the chair in front of it. Claire went to the kitchen and made her a cup of tea. When she came back Aunt Min's eyes were closed. Claire looked at her watch. The time was eleven o'clock.

After two or three minutes Aunt Min opened her eyes.

'Here's some tea for you,' Claire said.

'Thank you, Claire,' said Aunt Min. Her voice was weak. 'I'm a little better now.'

'You can't walk any more tonight,' said Claire.

'No, I don't think I can,' said her aunt.

'I'm going to find Mr Burge,' said Claire. 'Perhaps he can take us home in his car.'

Aunt Min looked worried. 'Where is he?' she asked.

'I think he's up at the castle,' said Claire.

'Claire, you can't –!' Aunt Min began to say.

'I know about the castle, Aunt Min,' said Claire. 'I'm not afraid.'

But she *was* afraid.

Chapter 4   The Black Tower

Walter Burge looked up at the Black Tower and thought he saw a light; but perhaps he didn't.

'I didn't see it,' he said.

He was afraid, and he knew it. He never went up to the castle at night. He never followed Alexa when she went out. He did not want to see or know the things that happened.

But things *did* happen, because Alexa was *more than a cat*.

22

Walter Burge looked up at the Black Tower and thought he saw a light; but perhaps he didn't.

Walter knew the story of Alexa, the witch with the fire-coloured hair. He knew it well. He read it when he was a boy. Then, ten years ago, the cat arrived at his cottage. Walter tried to send it away, but it came back again and again, and every time it came it went up to the castle. After some time Walter stopped trying to send the cat away. He gave it some food and called it Alexa because of its colour. After that, the cat made its home in Walter's cottage.

And then things began to happen.

Birds in the castle began to die. Somebody found a dead dog in one of the towers. A stone from the Black Tower fell on to a woman's head and killed her. A small boy from the village got lost in the castle and his father did not find him for three hours; after that day the boy never spoke again. Then people began to see lights and things moving up on the towers, but when they went to look, there was nothing there. Now the village people stayed away. And nobody ever went up to the castle at night.

Only Alexa.

But tonight Walter was there too. 'Alexa!' he called. 'Alexa!'

The wind took his words and carried them away.

♦

The orange cat sat on the tower. It saw the old man with the light in his hand. Then, far away, it saw another thing moving across the snow. *It was the girl!*

The cat was afraid of the girl. It watched her with its green eyes. Why did the girl come to the castle? What did she want?

♦

Claire followed Walter Burge's footprints in the snow.

The cat was afraid of the girl. It watched her with its green eyes.

'They're going up to the Black Tower,' she thought. 'But why?' And who went there before him?' She could see smaller footprints next to Walter's. 'Are they the footprints of a cat?'

She got to the bottom of the Black Tower and stopped. 'Mr Burge!' she called. But the wind was too strong for him to hear her.

'I could wait for him to come down,' she thought. But she remembered her aunt's tired face. 'No, Aunt Min must get home, so I must go and find him.'

The stairs were wet and difficult to see, and the wind was cold and strong. There was nothing to help her up the stairs, and her shoes were heavy with snow.

And then she saw the orange light at the top of the tower. Suddenly there was another sound, above the sound of the wind. What was it? Then she knew.

It was the sound of a fire, of burning.

Claire was very afraid. 'Go back down,' she told herself. 'Now!' But her feet didn't move.

Where was Walter Burge? Was he up there? His footprints went into the tower, but they did not come out again.

'Perhaps he's ill,' thought Claire. 'Perhaps he wants some help.' 'Mr Burge!' she called. 'Mr Burge!'

♦

Walter was inside a big orange light. He could not see through it. There was a fire, and he was in it, but he did not burn.

'Crazy!' he thought.

It was difficult to see in that light, but he could hear the sound. *Aaaaaagh!* The sound was outside his head and inside it at the same time.

'Alexa!' he called. 'Alexa! Stop! Stop this!'

Now he could hear another sound. Weaker. Quieter. What was it? A girl?

Walter was inside a big orange light.

'*Mr Burge . . . Mr Burge.*'

'Who is it?' he said. 'What's happening?'

'*It's Claire,*' the girl called.

'Claire? I don't know anybody called Claire,' he said. It was suddenly difficult to stand up. He put a hand on the tower wall.

Claire? *Claire?* He *did* know a Claire. Now who –?

And then he remembered! Claire was the name of the girl – the daughter of the man two hundred years ago at the castle. And she died because the witch did not help her. *Her* name was Claire. He remembered reading it in a book at the cottage.

'Claire?' he said. 'You're Claire? But Claire is dead.'

Some other thing said the name now. '*Claire . . .?*' Something near him. A woman? He could hear it. He could hear the name in the sound of the fire.

'*Claire? . . . Claire? . . . Claire?*'

The thing sounded very, very afraid.

'*Not dead? . . . Claire? . . . Not dead?*'

Suddenly the fire began to die and the orange light began to go out. Now Walter could see the sky above him and the tower round him.

'*Not dead? . . . Claire? . . . Not . . .?*'

Slowly the words died too.

Soon there was no fire, no sound. Only the light in Walter's hand.

♦

Claire went up the last of the stairs and out on to the top of the tower. She saw Walter Burge, but he did not hear her. He looked across the fields.

The orange-coloured cat sat on the wall of the tower. It saw Claire . . . *and its eyes were afraid*. It moved away from her.

Walter saw Claire's light. He turned quickly. Claire saw the stones behind him move.

'The wall!' she called.

Walter jumped away from the wall. His light fell from his hand and went out. The stones behind him fell into the night. Then half of the tower began to follow them.

Claire and Walter ran across to the stairs and down them. They looked back when they got to the bottom, when the sound of the falling stones stopped. Most of the Black Tower was suddenly not there.

They looked at it without speaking. Then Walter Burge said, 'We're lucky that we're not dead.'

'Yes,' said Claire. 'But . . . what happened to your cat?'

They found it in the snow at the bottom of the tower. It was dead.

Walter said nothing. He walked away sadly.

♦

Aunt Min opened her eyes when she heard them coming. Mr Burge came in first, then Claire.

'Mr Burge,' Aunt Min began. 'I . . . we –'

'The girl told me about the accident with the car,' said Walter.

Aunt Min looked at Claire. 'Are you all right?'

'Yes,' said Claire. Her face was white.

'Some of the tower fell down,' said Walter. 'The snow . . . it's very heavy . . .' He stopped.

Aunt Min looked at him, then looked back at Claire. 'I think I understand,' she said. And they knew that she did.

'I can take you home in my car,' said Walter.

'Thank you, Mr Burge,' said Aunt Min.

They went outside to Walter's car. The snow stopped falling when they opened the door.

The castle was different. Claire was not afraid of it now.

They sat in the back and Claire looked out of the window at the castle. It was different. She was not afraid of it now. The Black Tower wasn't tall now. Most of it was not there.

Claire looked at her watch; it was after midnight. 'It's Christmas Day,' she said. 'Happy Christmas, Aunt Min. Happy Christmas, Mr Burge.'

'Happy Christmas,' they said together.

♦

Walter walked up to the castle the next morning. He went to the bottom of the Black Tower and looked at the stones.

The fire-coloured cat was not there. He looked for it carefully, but it was not there.

And nobody ever saw the ghost of Genny Castle again.

ACTIVITIES

Chapters 1–2

Before you read

1 Look at the picture on page 3. What do you think of Genny Castle? Would you like to go there? Why or why not?

2 Find these words in your dictionary. They are all in the story. Do you understand all of them now?

   burn castle cottage crazy field ghost secret servant stone tower witch worry

   a Which two are people?
   b Which three could you make from stone?
   c Which could you see in the country, but not in the town?
   d Which word goes with *fire*?

3 Use one word to finish these sentences
   a 'I won't tell anybody. It will be our . . . . . .'
   b 'I think he's . . . . . He's always doing and saying stupid things.'
   c 'When you're late home I always . . . . . about you.'
   d 'I wouldn't go near that old house – my friend says she saw a . . . . . in there.'

After you read

4 How old is Claire?
5 Why is she staying with Aunt Min for Christmas?
6 What does Claire buy in the village shop?
7 What is Walter Burge wearing?
8 What do the village people think of Walter Burge?
9 The boy tells Claire the story of the Black Tower. Why does he think accidents happen there?
10 Where do these things happen?
   a Claire thinks she hears a bird
   b Claire finds the Christmas tree lights
   c Claire reads the book about Genny Castle

33

Chapters 3–4

Before you read

11 What do you think Claire will do next? Will she go to the castle again?

12 Why do you think Walter Burge called 'Stop!' to Claire?

13 Find the word *footprints* in your dictionary.
Make a sentence using these words:
snow / footprints / follow

After you read

14 Who said or thought these things?

    a 'Let's go across Walter Burge's field.'

    b 'Why did you go out on a night like this?'

    c 'We must stop here for you to sit down.'

    d 'I can see his footprints in the snow.'

15 How does Claire know that Walter Burge is in the tower?

16 What strange thing happens to Walter?

17 Are these sentences true (✓) or not true (✗)?
Change the words that are wrong

    a Aunt Min drives the car into a tree.

    b Walter is reading a book about cats.

    c Alexa pushes the cottage window open with her nose.

    d Claire and Aunt Min get into Walter's cottage through the back door.

    e Aunt Min hears the sound of burning.

    f They find the cat in the snow outside Walter's cottage.

Writing

18 Look again at the pictures in this book. Write two or three sentences about

    a Claire   **b** Aunt Min   **c** Walter Burge

19 The summer after this story ends, Claire stays with Aunt Min again. She visits Walter Burge one afternoon. Write their conversation.